LEADERS LIKE US

Grace Lee Boggs

BY KAREN SU

ILLUSTRATED BY
ARLO LI

T0021052

Rourke

Before Reading: *Building Background Knowledge and Vocabulary*

Building background knowledge can help children process new information and build upon what they already know. Before reading a book, it is important to tap into what children already know about the topic. This will help them develop their vocabulary and increase their reading comprehension.

Questions and Activities to Build Background Knowledge:

1. Look at the front cover of the book and read the title. What do you think this book will be about?
2. What do you already know about this topic?
3. Take a book walk and skim the pages. Look at the table of contents, photographs, captions, and bold words. Did these text features give you any information or predictions about what you will read in this book?

Vocabulary: *Vocabulary Is Key to Reading Comprehension*

Use the following directions to prompt a conversation about each word.

- Read the vocabulary words.
- What comes to mind when you see each word?
- What do you think each word means?

Vocabulary Words:
- *activist*
- *evolution*
- *grassroots*
- *immigrants*
- *perseverance*
- *PhD*
- *philosophy*
- *revolution*

During Reading: *Reading for Meaning and Understanding*

To achieve deep comprehension of a book, children are encouraged to use close reading strategies. During reading, it is important to have children stop and make connections. These connections result in deeper analysis and understanding of a book.

Close Reading a Text

During reading, have children stop and talk about the following:

- Any confusing parts
- Any unknown words
- Text to text, text to self, text to world connections
- The main idea in each chapter or heading

Encourage children to use context clues to determine the meaning of any unknown words. These strategies will help children learn to analyze the text more thoroughly as they read.

When you are finished reading this book, turn to the next-to-last page for **Text-Dependent Questions** and an **Extension Activity**.

TABLE OF CONTENTS

SEEDS OF ACTIVISM

Have you ever noticed something that could be changed for the better? Have you ever wanted to make a difference in people's lives? Grace Lee Boggs did. That's why she became an **activist**.

Grace was on her way home one day when she saw her neighbors marching in the street. They were protesting for better housing. Grace lived in a basement filled with rats, so the protest gave her hope. Seeing people fight for change affected her. She knew she had to join them.

Grace was born in 1915 in Providence, Rhode Island over her family's Chinese restaurant. Both of her parents were **immigrants**. Her mother had no schooling. She escaped a hard life in China as a girl. But she and Grace's father built a successful restaurant in New York City's Chinatown. Grace looked up to her parents. Their **perseverance** through hardship planted the seeds of her activism.

Grace was smart from a young age. At 16, she went to Barnard College. Grace turned to **philosophy** because other classes didn't make sense when the world needed changing. She was inspired by the ideas of philosophers she read about. Grace would come to especially like the philosophers Karl Marx and Friedrich Hegel. Hegel said that because reality is always changing, ideas have to change too. At 25, she earned her **PhD** from Bryn Mawr College.

FIGHTING FOR CHANGE

   After graduating, Grace had a hard time finding a job. No one would hire an Asian person to teach philosophy. Even department stores would not hire Asian people. She finally got a job at a library at the University of Chicago for very low pay.

   Grace had to find free housing. The living conditions in her building and neighborhood weren't good. Many of the homes were filled with rats. She didn't think anyone should have to live like that. She met Black activists in her neighborhood who felt the same way. She wanted to get involved in their cause.

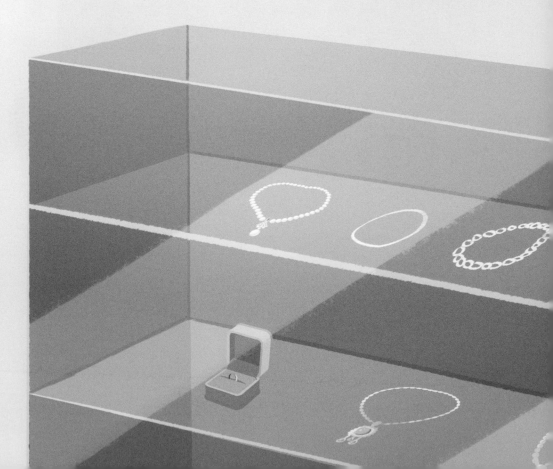

Grace moved to Detroit. She worked for a newsletter where she could write about her ideas. There she met James Boggs, known as Jimmy. He was an auto worker and he had the same ideas about change. Grace and Jimmy got married. They became important activists in Detroit. They fought for many causes, including workers' rights, civil rights, women's rights, and the environment.

They wrote books about their ideas. They even wrote one book together, **Revolution** and **Evolution** in the Twentieth Century. In 1992, they started Detroit Summer, a program for youth. The program helped young people get involved in their community. Grace and Jimmy's living room became a spot for activism in Detroit.

YOUNG PEOPLE GETTING CREATIVE
Young people in Detroit Summer use art, music, and poetry to express how community problems affect their lives. The program encourages them to become leaders and find solutions.

Grace and Jimmy were also active in the Black Power movement. The Black Power movement protested things such as police violence, loss of jobs, and failing schools. Grace and Jimmy helped organize protests and conferences with important leaders such as Malcolm X. One was a march down Woodward Ave. in Detroit 1963 where Dr. Martin Luther King Jr. spoke.

MARTIN AND MALCOLM

Martin Luther King Jr. and Malcolm X were both important civil rights leaders. Many think they were very different leaders, but Grace saw similarities between them. She saw them both grow and change their ideas as things changed around them.

GROWING SOLUTIONARIES

Jimmy died when Grace was 78, but Grace didn't stop fighting for change. She loved talking with people everywhere and listening to them. Grace's favorite question to ask was "what time is it on the clock of the world?" She believed people talking to each other is where the best ideas come from.

Grace wanted everyone to become a *solutionary*, or someone who tries to find solutions to help solve problems.

After so many years of movements and protests...
...Grace saw reality change...
...so Grace changed her ideas!

Instead of trying to make big changes, Grace focused on smaller changes. She saw hope in Detroit's people painting murals, planting community gardens and urban farms, and creating schools. She saw hope in small, local groups doing **grassroots** actions. She didn't want people to follow leaders. She wanted everyone to be leaders themselves.

Grace kept talking with people in her living room, making light bulbs go off in their heads. She sent people home with lots of books to read after they talked. She did this until the age of 100. In June 2015, the Detroit community held a big 100th birthday party for Grace. They celebrated her life's work before she died that October.

Today, programs such as Detroit Summer, the James and Grace Lee Boggs School, and the James and Grace Lee Boggs Center to Nurture Community Leadership continue to honor Grace and Jimmy. They are still helping people become solutionaries to change the world.

" We are the leaders we are looking for. "

–Grace Lee Boggs

TIME LINE

1915   On June 27, Grace Yu Ping Lee is born in Providence, Rhode Island to Chinese immigrant parents. Yu Ping means Jade Peace in Chinese.

1924   The Lees open Chin Lee restaurant in New York City's Chinatown.

1931   Grace attends Barnard College at age 16.

1940   Grace earns her PhD in philosophy from Bryn Mawr College.

1941   A philosophy library at the University of Chicago hires Grace when most places would not hire Asian people.

1941   Seeing protests for change makes Grace decide to become an activist. She moves to New York City to work with CLR James.

1953   Grace moves to Detroit, Michigan.

1963   Grace and Jimmy help organize a march in Detroit down Woodward Ave. where Dr. Martin Luther King Jr. speaks.

1974   Grace and Jimmy's book *Revolution and Evolution in the Twentieth Century* is published.

1992   Grace and Jimmy start Detroit Summer, a program for youth focusing on the arts and leadership.

1993   Jimmy dies.

1995   The James and Grace Lee Boggs Center to Nurture Community Leadership opens in Detroit.

2013   The James and Grace Lee Boggs school opens with a community-based philosophy.

2015   On October 5, Grace dies peacefully in Detroit.

GLOSSARY

activist (AK-tuh-vist): a person who takes actions to create change

evolution (ev-uh-LOO-shuhn): the gradual change into another form

grassroots (gras-ROOTS): the basic level of something, especially in relation to higher positions of power

immigrants (IM-i-gruhntz): people who move from one country to another and live there

perseverance (pur-suh-VEER-uhns): continued effort to do something and not giving up when things are difficult

PhD (pee-AYCH-dee): doctor of philosophy, the highest degree someone can earn from a graduate school

philosophy (fuh-LAH-suh-fee): the study of truth, wisdom, the nature of reality, and knowledge

revolution (rev-uh-LOO-shuhn): a radical change; this could be in government and who has ruling power, or a change of any kind that has great influence on the world

INDEX

TEXT-DEPENDENT QUESTIONS

1. Why did Grace decide to become an activist?

2. Who planted the seeds of activism in Grace?

3. What philosophers were important to Grace?

4. Why did Grace like to talk with people so much?

5. What grassroots actions gave Grace hope?

EXTENSION ACTIVITY

What is a world problem you would like to help solve? Write down the problem. Then write a plan for how you could be a solutionary for that problem. What would you have to learn? Who are people you would talk and work with?

ABOUT THE AUTHOR

Karen Su is a professor of Global Asian Studies at the University of Illinois Chicago. She has taught Grace Lee Boggs in her classes to inspire hope in her students. She also encourages them to learn from Boggs and become creative solutionaries to change the world for the better.

ABOUT THE ILLUSTRATOR

Arlo Li is an illustrator originally from China and now based in the US. He enjoys creating bright, whimsical, and colorful illustrations and specializes in children's books. He seeks to tell stories through his work and uses tiny details to bring those stories to life. He loves bringing his unique artistic vision to every project he works on.

© 2023 Rourke Educational Media

All rights reserved. No part of this book may be reproduced or utilized in any form or by any means, electronic or mechanical including photocopying, recording, or by any information storage and retrieval system without permission in writing from the publisher.

www.rourkebooks.com

PHOTO CREDITS: page 20: (C) Quyen Tran from the film American Revolutionary: The Evolution of Grace Lee Boggs (directed by Grace Lee)

Quote source: Grace Lee Boggs and Scott Kurashige. *The Next American Revolution: Sustainable Activism for the Twenty-First Century*, University of California Press, Berkeley, 2011, pp. 159, 178.

Edited by: Hailey Scragg
Illustrations by: Arlo Li
Cover and interior layout by: J.J. Giddings

Library of Congress PCN Data

Grace Lee Boggs / Karen Su
(Leaders Like Us)
ISBN 978-1-73165-630-8 (hard cover)
ISBN 978-1-73165-603-2 (soft cover)
ISBN 978-1-73165-612-4 (e-book)
ISBN 978-1-73165-621-6 (e-pub)
Library of Congress Control Number: 2022941708

Rourke Educational Media
Printed in the United States of America
01-0372311937